Dog Breeding:

A Guide to Mating and Whelping

Kay White

D0927610

John Bartholomew & Son Limited
Edinburgh

First published in Great Britain 1980 by
JOHN BARTHOLOMEW & SON LIMITED,
12 Duncan Street, Edinburgh, EH9 1TA.

ISBN 0 7028 1059 2

1st edition 1980
Reprinted 1983, 1984

British Library Cataloguing in Publication Data

White, Kay
    Dog Breeding
    1. Dogs - Breeding
    I. Title
636.7'08'2   SF427.2

Printed in Great Britain by
John Bartholomew & Son Limited

Contents

Dog Breeding in the Modern World

It would be all too easy for a newcomer to dog breeding to believe that there is no problem in getting a dog and bitch to mate, that whelping is simple and natural, and that puppies are reared with very little trouble. This may have been the picture when dogs were able to lead a much more natural existence — eating the skin and fur of freshly caught prey, as well as the flesh, and taking all the exercise needed to keep themselves well muscled, lean and agile. In addition, in earlier times many dogs were kept for their working ability, so that they used their talents and their brains to the full. Although the dogs of 50 years ago were unprotected against epidemic disease, they were probably more physically and mentally fit for breeding than the dogs of today.

The domestication of dogs has now reached such a peak that some members of the species have suffered a decline in virility. The current wave of anti-dog feeling means that many pets live very restricted lives with less than ideal exercise facilities and little opportunity for arousal by the opposite sex. Fashion has brought dogs whose physique is adapted to life in kennel and stable right into the fireside, e.g. the Old English Sheepdog and the Labrador. Fashion has brought dogs from Tibet, the Arctic and the tropics to live in our temperate climate and in centrally heated homes. Fashion has in the last 100 years formulated many new breeds to man's design; many of these dogs were put together for specific employment but now they are out of work and spend all their days in enforced idleness. I think of the Boxers, Dobermans and Rottweilers who should be working police and army dogs, the Jack Russell terriers bred to be superb ratters, and the many lovely Irish Setters that are frustrated because they will never know a day's cross-country work. Mentally and physically many pet dogs are not fit to breed from, although their health may be adequate for the lives they lead.

Our pedigree dogs are now very complex animals, and those who seek to breed puppies fit to sell must arm themselves with knowledge not only on the breed but about the genus of the dogs in general. Even to the old hands every litter is a separate and distinct event which brings its own problems; but every litter is also a fascinating experience.

If you go into dog breeding be aware that as a pastime it is not simple, nor financially rewarding, nor free from worry and grief. It can be full of heartbreak, it can be fun, but please do not undertake dog breeding light-mindedly.

If you decide to breed from your bitch, your two best friends will be your veterinary surgeon and the person from whom you bought the bitch, who is at least one litter ahead of you. Use these two experts in their separate ways; the vet for all things physical and help at whelping time and for any disease-condition that occurs in bitch and puppies. The breed expert can advise you on choosing a stud-dog, on breed idiosyncracies like length of pregnancy, and also about the state of the selling market in your breed.

In 1980 puppy sales are buoyant in *limited numbers.* You may place six labradors in the right homes in your locality, but a litter of ten would probably be too many and your last four puppies might well hang on far beyond the optimum selling time. This is a two-edged disaster, as puppies fit better into new homes around the eight-week stage and they become expensive for you to house and feed if you keep them too long. The larger the breed, the stronger is the buyer's impulse to have them really tiny; I have had Boxers turned down as too old at three months when they are becoming leggy and boisterous.

In breeds that habitually have large litters you will have to steel yourself to have excess puppies put down at birth. With the large breeds you should choose to keep bitches, as there is greater demand for these. It is never an easy thing to destroy healthy puppies and it is sometimes difficult to persuade a vet that it must be done, but he does not have your selling problem to cope with. Puppies *are* easy to sell and all too easy to buy, but unfortunately many people regard them as disposable and will get rid of them just as easily again. Eventually they become some of the thousands that are destroyed by rescue homes every year. If you care about what happens to your puppies you will under rather than over-estimate the number for which you can find good, permanent, caring homes, and you will place no reliance at all on those friends who said they would take puppies if ever you bred from your bitch; their lives may have changed in the interim.

Unfortunately the multi-puppy breeds, the German Shepherds, Afghans, Boxers and Setters, tend to be the most demanding adolescents to live with so you will have to be very sure of your customers before you rear more than six puppies in these breeds. As a concerned breeder you will want to sell your puppies yourself to individual homes. Selling by the litter to a dealer is quite unacceptable to those who care about the puppies they have caused to be born and means that you will never have the pleasure of seeing your puppies as they grow up.

In America there are many areas where breeding dogs is totally forbidden. In Britain if you own more than two breeding bitches from which you sell puppies, you must apply to the local authority for a licence to breed, which may cost from £2 to £20 a year, the amount being fixed by the local authority. Your premises will be inspected for suitability for the purpose by a person appointed by the local authority, possibly a veterinary surgeon, but more likely an Environmental Health Officer. These inspectors tend to have different viewpoints — the vet watching for health, comfort and convenience of the bitches — the environmental health man looking more at waste disposal, food storage and neighbourhood nuisance. Failure to get a 'Breeding of Dogs Act' licence will result in prosecution, for local authorities do watch the sales columns in local newspapers to monitor the breeders in their area.

Your household will be disrupted for at least eight weeks after a litter is born, so it is very important to allocate enough room for the whelping and the puppies; in a really crowded home it may not be possible to find a warm secluded place where the bitch may whelp and stay for the first three weeks. Seclusion is necessary, even for the most gregarious bitch as she should be encouraged to behave in the way her primitive ancestors would have and stay with her puppies continually for the first 21 days, except for short trips to be clean. Psychologically many pet bitches are torn between natural maternal behaviour, and their learned behaviour, which includes being busy around the house and greeting visitors. She must have comfort but she must not be in a busy kitchen or a hall where there are constant distractions and visitors. After the first three weeks you will want bitch and puppies to begin to socialize and to be where they can experience people and household noises. Around five weeks, if the weather is good, you may want to let the puppies enjoy themselves outdoors; it is essential that they have light, air and sunshine. Once the pups begin to move around they must have a generous space to live for this encourages them to be clean from the start and makes future housetraining much easier, and they must have room to play and exercise their limbs. Most people utilize a spare bedroom or study for the whelping and then move the puppies to a fenced-off enclosure in a ground-floor room. Later, as they grow, they can be placed in an insulated kennel and run in the garden. Growing puppies spoil furnishings and flower borders, so always try to enclose them, but let them be where they can see and be seen.

Eight week old puppies in playpen in the garden for a few hours in good weather. Note provision of water, shade, toys and sleeping box for protection from wind

The Dog and the Bitch

Most male dogs are sexually mature and capable of mating a bitch when ten months old. Some are ready at six months but may not be fertile until later. Not all dogs however are interested in mating bitches. This is partly caused by fashion, for in keeping male dogs in domestic situations we tend to select for docility and a tractable nature — temperaments that do not often accompany an aggressive sexual drive.

While it might seem an attractive idea to mate your bitch with a friend's dog of the same breed, you are giving yourself quite a formidable handicap unless your friend is knowledgeable about the breed, and the dog has been proved at stud. If you go to a professional stud-dog he will have been trained in his work, you will be able to see puppies by him, and his owner will more likely than not be able to help you in many ways, possibly even directing enquiries for puppies your way. The more of a beginner to the art of breeding that you are, the more you will need the help of an experienced dog-owner. You will find the professional stud-dogs with their owners at any big dog-show, and the names of both in the weekly dog papers and directories. The Kennel Club will also provide you with a list of prominent people in the breed in which you are interested. Possibly the easiest way to make contact is to return to the kennels from which you bought your bitch puppy and ask their frank advice in picking a suitable sire.

In choosing your stud-dog you will probably have in mind the colour and shape you prefer, bearing in mind that you should not select a dog that has features exactly opposite those you see in your bitch. Your bitch may have too long a nose for strictly classical beauty, but it would be a mistake to take her to a dog with an exaggerated flat face. Similarly with body-size, do not mate a very

9

small to an over-large specimen, but rather to one that is just the right size for the breed. The age of the sire does not matter, provided that he is not really aged in terms of the life-span of the breed.

Veterinary knowledge is growing continually and we now know that many breeds of dogs are plagued with such hereditary diseases are epilepsy, a malformation of the hip joint known as Hip Dysplasia, a deformation of the knee joint known as Luxating Patella, and many forms of progressive blindness, of which the best-known is Progressive Retinal Atrophy (P.R.A.). In Britain a panel of veterinary opthalmologists has been appointed to examine dogs for P.R.A., Hereditary Cataract, and Collie Eye Anomaly. Your local veterinary surgeon can arrange this examination for you. You must take the pedigree and official Kennel Club registration papers with you so that the dog may be positively identified. The onset of P.R.A. occurs at different ages in different breeds, so that interim certificates are granted when it is desirable to breed before the age when a final clearance certificate can be given.

The official assessment of Hip Dysplasia (H.D.) status cannot take place until the dog is over 12 months old as up till that time there will be growth changes. The dog must be X-rayed under full anaesthetic as positioning of the spine and hind-legs is extremely important. The dog's Kennel Club registration number must be photographed onto the X-ray plate. A local veterinary surgeon will take the X-ray and then submit it, with the appropriate fee, to an official panel of scrutineers, all orthopaedic surgeons, who work in a group of three in order to arrive at a balanced opinion.

The British criteria for H.D. status are the most stringent in the world, and a dog which obtains a pass in Britain will almost certainly do so in any other country.

Not all breeds are routinely examined for H.D. Bulldogs, Basset Hounds and all the toy breeds are not suitable for submission. H.D. is regarded as an especially important fault in the German Shepherd Dog, the Briard, the Old English Sheepdog, Labrador, Rottweiler and other working breeds.

Eye disease is an important fault in all types of Collie, Labradors, Sheepdogs, Briards, Poodles, Cockers and Tibetan Terriers.

Kennel clubs all over the world are equally concerned about eliminating eye disease and improving abnormalities of the hip joint, and each runs its own schemes with which veterinary surgeons will be familiar.

A good way of finding out what problems currently concern breeders of your breed is to join the appropriate breed club (addresses can be obtained from The Kennel Club), and to read its literature with care and thought. Most clubs publish a bulletin and there is a tendency to organize instructive lectures and 'teach-ins' during the winter months. The clubs will also inform you of symposia run by commercial companies, usually with very little reference to their own products and always with the aim of allowing the veterinary profession to meet and talk to dog-owners and breeders. There is a tremendous amount to learn about a dog before you give thought to producing puppies to which someone has to give a home.

The search for a stud-dog can begin quite early, when your bitch is over her first season perhaps. You may change your mind several times about the dog of your choice, but this is all to the good as you will be learning all the time about the type you prefer and the attributes of the breed you have chosen to make your own.

However, before you finally set your heart on breeding a litter, there is quite a lot of additional information that you need to know about your bitch. Was she one of your average-size litter? Did her dam whelp easily and normally? Whelping ability is strongly hereditary and your worst prospect would be to attempt to breed from a singleton puppy, born by caesarean, whose mother refused to feed her. If you find that your bitch's history is in any way similar to this it would be better not to consider producing a litter, as it could prove to be an expensive heartbreak. For although many people buying pet puppies will say they have no objection to taking one with a major fault, provided it causes no pain, e.g. you may not mind that your Cavalier King Charles Spaniel has an undershot mouth or light-coloured eyes, although both these attributes are regarded as faults in the breed. Even if she is the most lovely pet, it is not a good idea to breed on from such a faulty bitch as a proportion of the pups will carry the same faults and thus a breed begins to degenerate. It is a sound idea to take your bitch back to her breeder and to ask whether such an animal is suitable to breed from.

If you have decided that dog breeding is for you, consult your vet about the use of the hormone 'Pill' or injections of progesterone to postpone or eliminate any of your bitch's heat-periods, as these hormones can have long-lasting effects. If the bitch has been treated for a mismating, or an early abortion has been brought about, it is as well to wait for a whole year before planning a litter.

Most bitches are ready for mating at the second heat (season, oestrus period), provided they are mature in mind and body. Some giant breeds are better left until they are over two years, while people involved in the smallest toy breeds think it better to mate their bitches at the first heat, which may occur in any breed at between 5–6 months to over 18 months. The normal interval between heats is said to be six months but there is such wide variation in individual bitches that anything between 7 and 10 months is very common. The interval between first and second heat is usually the one the bitch will reproduce for life, except when she has had a litter at a previous heat, when the following one is usually delayed. Heat-periods may occur at less than six-month intervals, but this is a warning that all may not be well with the bitch's reproductive system and I would have such a bitch checked by a vet. Sometimes slightly stepping up the protein content of a bitch's diet will seem to bring into season a young bitch that is proving tardy, especially at the first heat; I give extra red meat at such times.

Bitches used to be said to come into season in early spring and early autumn, but domestication has changed all that, especially for dogs that live in the house and enjoy warm conditions and prolonged lighting. Kennel dogs that are put to bed at dusk are more likely to remain close to the natural timing, but house bitches 'come in' at any time of year, and frequently trigger off others in the house to be in season, probably through scent stimulation. The earliest sign is a heightened sensitivity, perhaps irritability or high spirits. The external genital organ, the vulva, enlarges and softens. Internally during this time, the surface of the bitch's long vagina will be changing and tiny blood vessels will become enlarged. Finally they will rupture and you will see a blood-stained discharge

Normal Vulva of bitch   Enlarged Vulva of bitch

from the vulva. The time from the first signs of actual blood-stained discharge may be only a few days or as much as eight weeks.

During the first part of the bitch's season, from the first day she shows colour, until she ovulates at around the 12th–14th day, very definite cell changes can be found on the vagina walls and around the cervix and if a bitch has proved difficult to mate at an earlier season your veterinary surgeon can help you to find the optimum day by taking smears from the vagina and examining them for cell type under a microscope. Several of these tests may be necessary on successive days before the right day for the mating is found, so it is an expensive technique only suitable for use when it has not been found possible to get a fruitful mating otherwise.

Changes are also taking place in the ovaries, uterus and vagina before the bitch starts to bleed (show colour), during the heat and after the heat is over. Nature has planned that the normal bitch will be willing to mate with the dog just before she ovulates, that is, sheds the ova (eggs) which his sperm will fertilize. We say that the right time for a canine mating is between the 10th and 14th days but individual bitches are capable of great variation, some being ready very early in the heat and others standing to be mated after the three weeks that we normally allow as the heat-period has passed. The most common error is to take a bitch to the stud too early, before she is physically and psychologically ready. She will refuse, in no uncertain terms, to be mated. Bitches will often simulate mating play with each other before they are willing to allow a dog to mate them.

It is only possible to get a coupling with a bitch that is not ready by the exertion of considerable physical force on the part of the owners, and there is little chance that such a mating will be fertile; it is also very cruel to the bitch.

Inevitably the variation in mating day may mean that you have to make more than one visit to the stud, not being too disappointed if the first time is not successful. An abortive visit is however useful in accustoming the bitch to the dog and the owners to the mating routine. Very often a second visit in 24—36 hours will bring about a mating with very little trouble.

PARENTS	GRAND – PARENTS	G. G. – PARENTS
SIRE Champion Seefeld Goldsmith. (Red/white).	**SIRE** Champion Seefeld Picasso.	**SIRE** Gl. Seefeld Holbein
		DAM Gl. Seefeld Musk Rose.
KENNEL CLUB STUD NO: 3568 BT. **OWNER:** Mr S. Somerfield.	**DAM** Cherrybuxton Fine Art	**SIRE** Gl. Casparlain Opus Too.
		DAM Hildorf Honeypot.
DAM Duckscottage Mixed Blessing (Red).	**SIRE** Duckscottage the Tigger.	**SIRE** Radden Upper Crust.
		DAM Tabitha of Duckscottage
KENNEL CLUB STUD NO: B 67427107. **OWNER:** Kay White	**DAM** Balmoral Blossom.	**SIRE** Duckscottage Fabulous
		DAM Duckscottage Zany.

NAME OF PUPPY: Duckscottage Mimosa
KENNEL PREFIX: Duckscottage
BREED: Boxer
SEX: Bitch
COLOUR: Red/white
DATE OF BIRTH: 19.2.1980
KENNEL CLUB NO: Registration Applied for.
OWNER: Mrs E. Bailey
ADDRESS: The Laurels, Treetop Hill, Dorking, Surrey

I certify this Pedigree to be correct to the best of my knowledge
Signed: Kay White.
Date: 16.6.80

Dog pedigree form

Stud Procedure

It is usual, though by no means obligatory, for the bitch to visit the dog, as a male is less inhibited in his behaviour on his own territory. Sometimes if the two live far apart it is possible to meet half-way, at another kennels or in some secluded piece of country where the mating can be performed after the dogs have been taken for a walk together. Some professional stud-dogs however are so sure of themselves that they will travel to the home of the bitch.

Matings are best and most naturally performed out-of-doors where dog and bitch can have a good run together, perform their natural sequence of mating play, and become sexually excited in the course of the game. Sometimes outdoor play is impossible and the pair should then be allowed as much freedom as possible in a garage or room where they can run about. The practice of mating dog and bitch with maximum human involvement, but almost no freedom for the canine pair, has been found to be the basis of much infertility. The desire to stage-manage matings so that very little time need be spent by the owners reached such a pitch a few years ago that it was customary to take a bitch into a room, muzzle her to prevent biting, possibly put her on a table, lower the dog onto her back, and get him to perform the mating act with no preliminary play, but possibly with manual stimulation by his owner. In this way it was possible to complete a perfunctory coupling, extract a cheque from the bitch's owner, and see them on their way again in 30 minutes.

Twenty years ago it was usual to send a bitch, unaccompanied, by train to spend a few days at the kennels of the stud-dog, where she would be kept until one or two matings had been accomplished. Then the bitch would be returned to her owners by the same route by which she came. This method had disadvantages.

There was room for deception, since the dog paid for was not necessarily the one used; or the bitch arrived in a frightened and disturbed condition with the concomitant high levels of adrenalin in her body which modern research has shown inhibit fertility. We now know that we must expect to spend quite a lot of time and trouble to get a bitch mated and that if we are not able to do this, it is not worthwhile to think of breeding dogs.

You may find that there are still stud-dog-owners who want to arrange hurried forced matings, or will ask you to send the bitch unaccompanied. Their case may perhaps be justified in that stud fees are in most breeds so low, possibly only a quarter to half the cost of a pedigree puppy in the breed. If stud fees were equal to the cost of one puppy, which is now up to £100 in popular breeds and much more in rare ones, the stud-owner might be willing to give more time and trouble to achieving a happy coupling for the dogs.

A mating is always rather a tense business in that both dog and bitch owner hope it will go well, but cannot in the end force the inclinations of dog and bitch. Bitches are known to have individual preferences for dogs of their own choice and while resisting the overtures of Champion will return to their home only too eager to get themselves mated to the black Labrador waiting in the garden. Parents sometimes think that the mating of the family bitch will be very useful as a biological demonstration, and I have even known children be kept from school specially to attend a mating. It is unfair to expect the stud-owner to have to cope with childish questions and comments when there is a job to be done. A mating is a serious business; your first step on the way to breeding a litter. It is not an entertainment, nor should it be an embarrassment to either owner.

The custom in the canine world is to pay an outright fee for the mating on the day it is performed. The custom of taking a pick-of-the-litter puppy has almost died out and there is little to recommend its revival as so much bad feeling was often the outcome. The stud fee is paid regardless of whether puppies result, although most stud-owners will agree to let the bitch come again at the next heat provided they are informed at once after the pregnancy period that no pups have been born. If puppies are born and subsequently die before selling age, the stud-dog's obligations have been technically discharged. If only one puppy is born the dog has been proved fertile and it is usual to 'blame' the bitch for the litter size. Many stud-dog-owners are very generous however and will often allow another mating, or one at half-price, if you have had bad luck, as they are professionally anxious for the reputation of their stud to be maintained. But it is not at all common for the stud fee to be returned in cash, should you decide that dog breeding is not for you after all.

The stud fee is payable immediately after a satisfactory mating is completed. In exchange the bitch's owner should receive a copy of the dog's pedigree with Kennel Club number, and copies of any signed forms that may be necessary to register the litter. It is also important that you receive photocopies of any certificates of freedom from eye disease or from Hip Dysplasia which have been awarded to the dog. It has happened that people have been misled by advertisements that claim, for example, 'All stock X-rayed for Hip Dysplasia' into thinking that all the dogs have been certified as free from H.D. Check that any such certificates shown bear the Kennel Club number of the dog that served your bitch. Make sure that you also keep a signed copy of any agreement made about a return service in case the bitch should miss. It is usual to say that such a return shall be at the next heat and to the same dog. If he is no longer available, or if you want to wait until a further heat, then you are asking for a concession from the stud-owner, not a right.

It is preferable to allow bitch and dog to get acquainted before mating

Bitch and stud dog enjoying premating play

The bitch is mounted by the stud dog

The Mating

You should begin to get your bitch in top condition for breeding long before the proposed time for mating. Check with the Kennel Club or the appropriate controlling society that her registration is as required for a brood bitch, so that her puppies will be eligible for registration. If the bitch is overweight, slim her down and give her plenty of exercise to bring her into good muscular condition to make whelping easier. Any irritable skin conditions or digestive faults should be cleared up on veterinary advice, for pregnancy and whelping can only make such diseases worse and perhaps pass them on to another generation. Special care should be taken that the bitch's ears are free of mites and also that any other dogs or cats in the household are free of skin diseases and fleas.

The bitch should receive any vaccination boosters against distemper, hardpad and leptospirosis that will fall due in the next four months, so as to pass on the maximum amount of maternal antibody to her pups. Boosters given during pregnancy may adversely affect the puppies and after whelping is too late for the pups to benefit. It does no harm to worm the bitch just before mating day, although in a well-kept animal you are unlikely to see any roundworms passed.

Get the bitch on to a feeding routine that she accepts and on which she passes regular well-formed excreta. Study the analysis of the food used and supply vitamins A, B, D and E if they are not included in the food; many tinned meats and processed foods contain all necessary vitamins and minerals. It is not known whether vitamin C is needed by dogs, but there is no harm in giving rose-hip syrup. It is far easier to give a well-balanced multi-vitamin/mineral preparation made by a reputable and famous manufacturer than to attempt to balance cod-liver oil, calcium and bone-flour each day, and many dogs object to having these substances put on their dinners. I prefer to give tablets, which dogs will eat eagerly and which can be treated as rewards and titbits, so I use one containing vitamin D (as found in cod-liver oil) and phosphorus/calcium in the correct ratio to form the puppies' skeletons, and other tablets for vitamin B. Similar tablets can be broken up for the puppies as soon as they start weaning.

Many breeders think that a course of vitamin E tablets is an aid to fertility; if you wish to give them, start well before mating day. The tablets in varying strength may be bought from health shops and chemists.

Watch the bitch closely for signs that she is coming into season. It is important to notice the first day she shows the blood-stained discharge from the vulva, for this is your starting point for the calculation of mating day. It is wise to test the vulva with a white tissue morning and evening, as many bitches keep themselves clean and may be able to conceal the flow for a few days and so will throw you out in your calculations. A minority of bitches have what is known as a colourless season when no red discharge at all is present, and yet the bitch becomes ready for mating and may be fertile. A colourless season is an abnormality and it is doubtful whether it is wise to perpetuate it by breeding from such a bitch. If you decide to do so you can only judge the correct mating day by the size and expansion of the vulva and the amount of sexual excitement the bitch is exhibiting.

On the first day the bitch shows colour, telephone the stud-owner to make a tentative appointment for the 11th, 12th or 13th day according to the breed. The appointment must be flexible as the only object is to suit the bitch. It follows that you may wish to limit your choice of stud-dog to one that you can easily visit several times. It may seem attractive to plan to meet your chosen dog at a dog-show, but the Kennel Club have considered this and have expressly forbidden mating in the precincts of any show, whether held indoors or out.

The custom is gradually returning of making two visits to the stud, 48 hours apart, for a mating of maximum fertility, possibly on the 11th and 13th days, or on the 12th and 14th. While waiting for the right day to come round, take special care that no stray dog jumps into the garden or even through a window into the house. For several days before the mating, leave off any scented preparations or tablets you may have been using to discourage the attention of other dogs.

On the mating day do not feed the bitch; but do all you can to soothe her if she is upset by travelling, and avoid arriving in a state of fuss. Allow the bitch to empty her bladder just before arriving at the stud's home, but *not* just outside, so that all the males in the neighbourhood come to add to it. Bring the bitch in on a strong collar and lead, and in case you have to hold or support her during the mating, make sure that you are wearing practical clothing.

The stud-dog's owner stages the mating procedure. This should include some free play in which dog and bitch make stylized passes at each other in a special manner not seen at any other time. The dog's owner will know if the play is leading up to mating or whether success is unlikely that day. Most professional studs are very clever in allowing their bitches just enough flirtation and refusal before calling their bluff. You will notice that the eager bitch is standing with her tail turned to one side and the vulva uptilted. The dog mounts her back, and clutching her around the ribs with his fore-paws, enters the vulva with his penis. It is at this stage that many owners like to move in to guide the dog and to steady the bitch so that she cannot move away. It may be necessary to kneel down to support the bitch under her abdomen so that she does not collapse under the weight of the dog, and if the bitch is emotionally keyed up, it may be necessary to tie her muzzle lightly to prevent her from nipping helpers or indeed the dog. Much has been written about the possibility of dog and bitch harming each other at mating time but I have never seen it happen. A bitch who does not intend to be mated is usually so emphatic about it that the dog decides not to approach her.

The dog will make thrusting movements as he produces his ejaculation in three phases; the first a lubricating emission to clear the penis of urine, then the sperm-bearing fraction, and finally a copious amount from the prostate to wash the sperm up towards the bitch's cervix. This fraction contains no sperm, so the old-fashioned practice of standing the bitch up on her front feet, to allow the final secretions to drain in, is a complete waste of effort.

After ejaculation the dog will dismount and turn himself, with or without human assistance, until the pair stand back to back in the tie

The tie may last from a few minutes to over an hour, but twenty minutes is an average time

The ejaculatory part of the mating will be over in two to three minutes and the sperm is then on its way to meet the egg.

Now there should come the 'tie', a phenomenon unique to the dog and its near-relations. The bulb of the dog's penis has become engorged with blood and enlarged considerably. The newly corrugated surface of the bitch's vagina helps to hold the penis in place and the two become locked together for anything up to one hour. As the bitch would be unable to bear the dog's weight on her back for so long, he turns himself or is turned by the handlers so that his penis is bent back on itself and the pair are back to back, held on leads so that they cannot pull each other around. The tie is undoubtedly a promising sign at mating, but matings can be fertile without a tie provided dog and bitch have been in contact long enough for sperm to be introduced. With large dogs it is hardly possible to fake a tie, but with tiny dogs it is possible to hold the pair closely together as if they were locked. A proper tie maintains itself and the pair need only be restrained at the front end. Unless the tie goes on for nearly an hour, no attempt should be made to break it artificially, and this applies to mismatings too. An unduly long tie when both human and dogs are getting bored may be eased by the application of smooth slivers of ice to the bitch's vagina. During the tie some bitches cry or grumble; it is an emotional reaction and does not mean they are being hurt. Some will twist themselves about in an effort to get free, so they must be steadied, but a perfect mating between well-matched parties can be performed with absolutely no human interference from first meeting to breaking from the tie, if the dogs are uninhibited and the owners do not fuss them.

Should a dog fail to complete a mating, probably because the bitch threw him off at the wrong moment, he should be taken away and rested, and another attempt made two hours later.

The perfectly performed mating does not prove that the male is fertile. He may have the right inclinations but no sperm, or sperm of poor quality — sperm unable to swim or to move in a purposeful direction. All these disabilities may overtake a proven stud at some time in his life, but it will not be found out until several bitches have missed having puppies by him. Over use is now not thought to affect the stud's fertility so much as stress, mental upset and advancing age, or a viral disease.

When the tie is finally broken both dog and bitch will lick their sexual organs to clean them up, and the bitch may go home if she is a good traveller or be rested for an hour or two at the kennels, as her owner wishes.

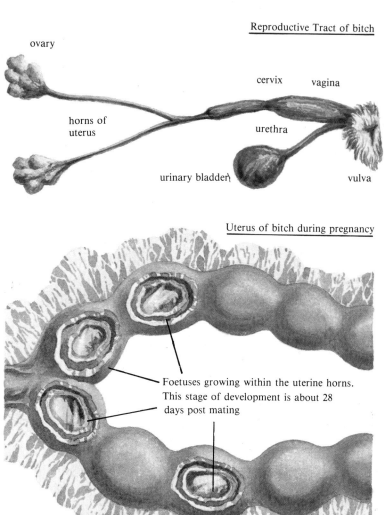

Reproductive Tract of bitch

ovary

cervix   vagina

horns of
uterus

urethra

urinary bladder

vulva

Uterus of bitch during pregnancy

Foetuses growing within the uterine horns.
This stage of development is about 28
days post mating

After the Mating

Thousands of male sperm will live within the bitch for up to a week, perhaps even more, so that they are well positioned to fertilize the ova coming down from the ovaries via the fallopian tubes. The bitch may not ovulate for 48 hours or more and will give no external sign of having done so. The fertilized egg will not become embedded in the wall of the uterus until about 9−10 days after the mating. Where the egg attaches to the side of the twin long-balloon-shaped uterine horns, you have the cells that will grow into the placenta through which the developing puppy will be nourished. When the puppy is ready to be born and has finished with the placenta it will be expelled with, or just after, the puppy (the afterbirth). This blood-filled tissue is usually eaten by the bitch, providing her with a lot of easily digested nourishment at a time when, in the wild, she would be unable to fend for herself. Pregnancy in the bitch used to be said to last for a flat 63 days in all breeds, but a recent survey by the Polish Kennel Club has revealed a great diversity in the duration of gestation, showing that some breeds take a lot longer and some less than 63 days. This is important knowledge as timing may be crucial when deciding if a litter needs to be removed by caesarean section.

In the following list of popular breeds and durations of pregnancy, marked differences are revealed: Boxer 63.5; Doberman 62.8; Dane 62.8; Fox Terrier 62.6; Dachshund 62.5; Alsatian (German Shepherd Dog) 62.1; Poodle 62.5; Peke 61.4.

The range is roughly between 54 and 72 days with 10 per cent of bitches whelping before the 60th day.

For the first five weeks of pregnancy no extra food should be given nor any alteration made to normal procedure, but you should be taking extra care of your bitch in subtle ways. She should be specially guarded against picking up infection, for when puppies are born dead or deformed, this can often be attributed to a minor viral infection picked up in early pregnancy. I would avoid boarding her or taking her to dog-shows. If she is a working dog or takes part in obedience training she should not be put at scales or jumps after she has been mated. Exercise should be continued, as the well-exercised bitch has the least problems at whelping time.

You will be most anxious to know if your bitch is pregnant; a veterinary surgeon may be able to palpate the uterus and feel the tiny foetuses between the 21st and 28th days of pregnancy but not later. Pregnancy diagnosis is easier in the thin- and smooth-coated bitch and much harder in a breed like the Puli where there are four inches of matted coat to mask the outline. I do not bother with early pregnancy diagnosis, preferring to let my bitches tell me. Sometimes I misunderstand what they say, or they delude themselves that they are pregnant, but that all adds to the interest of breeding.

At about five weeks after mating you will notice some changes in the bitch. She may seem to have enlarged in width just behind the ribs and her teats have become more prominent and pink in colour. She may at this stage go off her food and be capricious about what she will eat. Some vomit a little white froth in the mornings. After this she may be asking for more food, but relatively little more except in the giant breeds. The average bitch will be wanting about a third more than normal, with vitamins and minerals in proportion. It does definite harm to overload her with vitamins, especially fish liver oil, so stick to the multivitamin preparation and give this in accordance with the makers' instructions. The extra food that you give should be largely in the form of protein with not too much bread or biscuits.

Any slight illness that occurs in the pregnant bitch should receive veterinary attention more quickly than you would seek it in normal times. Exercise should be kept up, except in very hot weather when it would be unwise to exhaust the bitch, and very rough play and fights must be severely discouraged.

Every bitch, whether mated or not, undergoes hormonal changes after her season, which mimic pregnancy to a greater or lesser degree. Some bitches go through most of the bodily changes and produce milk; they have mock whelping pains and mother some inanimate object instead of puppies. When they are guarding a litter which no one else can see they can be very snappy and undergo a total personality change for a week or so, but they do not keep the litter as long as a real one and are usually bored with the whole idea within a week. One can understand the irritability as the bitch must be very harassed when she is certain that she has puppies to care for and no one will acknowledge them, least of all other dogs.

It is not easy to distinguish the early stages of a phantom pregnancy from a real pregnancy, but a bitch really heavy in whelp with live puppies moving inside her is unmistakable. Where there are only one or two live pups high up under the ribs there may still be nothing to see. Phantom pregnancies may be treated by the vet with hormones but I prefer to give more exercise and rather less food and let my bitches work through the phase. A real pregnancy does nothing to stop the bitch having phantoms at subsequent heats; the only real cure is to have the bitch spayed.

Around the seventh week of pregnancy the heavily in-whelp bitch will show a definite change in outline; this is something that happens literally overnight and leaves you in no doubt that she is pregnant, as phantom pregnancies cannot simulate this change which is caused by the weight and size of the growing puppies. Externally you will see that the whole load has shifted downwards, leaving the bitch with hollow flanks and a protrusion low in the body. What has happened is that the size of the puppies and their placentae inside the horns of the uterus have distended that organ so much that it cannot be accommodated and has to fold back on itself. This event seems to cause the bitch some discomfort and she may miss a meal or two at this time.

When this alteration has taken place there may be loss of appetite as the abdomen is so full that stomach capacity is reduced. Meals should be divided into three or four small amounts during the day. You may find that the grossly enlarged bitch is experiencing pressure on the bladder and she cannot remain clean at night. She will return to her former good habits once her maternity leave is over.

The pregnant bitch should be well fed and allowed as much

exercise as she wishes to take. Around the 50th day of pregnancy bone is laid down in the puppy skeletons and they will now show on X-ray.

Although the desire to verify that puppies are present and to guess how many there are is overwhelming, it is much better not to prod, push and handle the bitch too much or to let children play with her roughly or treat her in any way that may cause injury to the pups. Stressful situations should be avoided; e.g. she should not be taken in the car in hot weather or given the opportunity to plunge into icy water. Having already invested time and money in your litter it is only sensible to protect your investment and give the litter the best possible chance of being born fit and healthy.

It is important to tell any veterinary surgeon who treats your bitch for any condition at all that she may be pregnant. Medicines, ointments and shampoos left over from previous incidents should not be used as some drugs can have adverse effects on the developing puppies. In particular it is best to avoid insecticidal shampoos and sprays at this time and to keep the coat clean by brushing and washing, if necessary, with pure soap only. Take care that the bitch does not lick shampoo off her coat. One vomiting episode may do no harm at all but these things are best avoided. Towards the end of pregnancy a very distended bitch with a large litter on board may leak a little fluid from the vulva when she sits down. As long as it is only a small amount and the fluid is clear, there is no need to worry. During pregnancy the vulva may be slightly more moist than normal and may produce a slightly opaque discharge as whelping time draws near. This is quite normal; but for any heavy, blood-stained, or green-stained discharge you need veterinary advice on the same day that you notice it.

Sometimes bitches that have given every indication of being pregnant suddenly cease to look that way. It is now established that bitches can reabsorb their puppies, probably before any bone is laid down, so there will be nothing for you to see. The reason may be injury to the bitch, stress, or a high temperature due to a viral infection.

Abortion, i.e. the birth of the puppies well ahead of normal whelping time, before their development is completed, is uncommon in the bitch. It has only happened once in my kennel and that was after a seven and a half week pregnant bitch had a fight with her sister. The puppies were much too premature to live. You need help quickly if your bitch goes into labour very early.

Reproductive organs of male dog

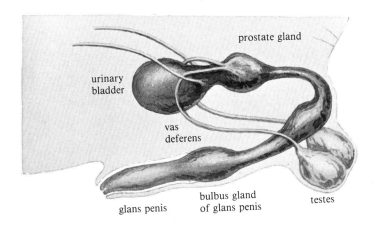

Bitch showing satisfactory signs of pregnancy.

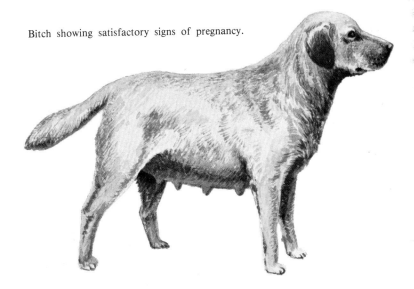

Foetuses implanted along the horns of the uterus

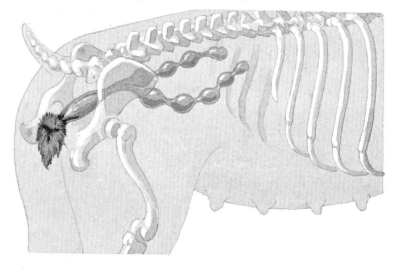

Foetus descending uterine horn

Puppy presenting hind first at cervix

Puppy obstructing across cervix

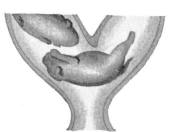

This puppy with extended foreleg may respond to manual extraction by veterinary surgeon

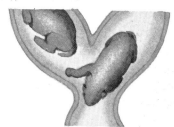

The Whelping Room

Once you are fairly sure, at the 5−6 week stage, that pups are on the way, you will want to gather all the equipment you will need to prepare the room. To remind you, the room must be warm, secluded, free of draught, easily cleaned, and capable of being darkened. For a small breed it is possible to screen-off a corner of a room in a part of the house not greatly used; for a large bitch you will need more space and quarters of more solid construction. For the first weeks after the birth she will be reluctant to leave her pups and if away from them, in a great hurry to get back, so she may be clumsy. For the larger breeds do not have screens that can be knocked over onto paraffin heaters or other hazards; and beware of overloading the electricity supply. Carpets should be taken up or covered, as the larger bitches lose a considerable amount of blood-stained discharge from the vulva for several weeks after whelping and they will drop and spot when they move about or sit down.

You will need a whelping box in which the bitch will produce and rear her puppies, and which will serve as a bed for them until they are sold. Research into whelping conditions has brought about a retreat from the open-tray-type box with an infra-red lamp suspended overhead; these lamps had many snags — they dried coats, were uncomfortable for the bitch, and provided warmth only directly under the lamp. Modern thought concentrates on creating a mini-environment for the bitch that is similar to the dug-out she would create for herself if wild. Many bitches do some very constructive digging in the garden in the last few days before whelping and some have succeeded in actually producing their puppies quite normally in places of their own creation.

The advantage of the mini-environment box is that it needs no

extra heating, just the normal room heat, so you are spared any anxiety as to whether the pups are too hot or not hot enough.

We have an insulated box with double sides, with a removable lid. The hole through which the bitch enters must be as small as possible so that with the lid on she has a mini-environment which conserves her own body heat. If the bitch needs more air, she lies with her head through the opening and seems to feel very secure and comfortable. The lid is removed during the whelping, so that the bitch can be helped if necessary, and for cleaning purposes later. Our box is made to take apart because made for a large dog it is quite bulky, but for small breeds the construction should be simplified by making the box in one piece. For the really small, light bitch a similar arrangement can be made from two large grocery cartons, one inside the other.

Clock to time intervals between births
Commercially formulated replica of bitch's milk
Torch. Necessary to check that bitch has not expelled a puppy or a placenta with urine
Glucose solution. 1 tablespoonful to 1 pint boiled water, for fluid therapy in ailing puppies
Lubricant Jelly for internal examination
Disinfectant in solution
Medical scrub solution for hands
Soft paper roll
Pen and book for record keeping
Low reading veterinary thermometer
Curved and pointed stainless steel scissors
Belcroy feeder for puppies
Bottle brush for cleaning bottle
Hand washing equipment if no running water available in whelping room

Bitches with huge coats like the Samoyeds and Keeshonds may want cooler conditions, so an open box without a lid will suit them, but the room should be capable of being darkened to a twilight state, most in keeping with natural conditions. Most bitches have great compulsion to stay with their puppies for the first two to three weeks after the birth, but you will not get the best feeding and mothering care if the bitch is uncomfortable, so you must be ready to monitor conditions in her room and to draw blinds, if for instance she is in full sun. Many people find it convenient to have a bitch whelp in a room extension that is largely glass. This can work well as long as it is remembered that these rooms heat up and also lose temperature quickly, and that people and other animals may peer in through the glass and make the bitch feel that her security is threatened. Even the most protected bitch feels vulnerable at this time, for she must realize that she is not fully fit to fight her own battles and has the necessity to protect her young family.

Most people like to sleep within earshot of the bitch for the last days before whelping and a few days after, in case she needs attention. Therefore, it is a good idea to choose a room capable of holding a camp-bed, a steady table, and a strong light for examination of the bitch, that is close to a source of hot water for convenience.

The whelping box is best made by a handyman or builder but it may be that in the future a box made to my pattern may be commercially available. The box needs to be a little longer than the bitch fully stretched out lying down, and rather deeper than her height. I have discarded the whelping rail or creep which used to be a feature of boxes as I found that puppies could get trapped under these rails and become chilled through not being able to feed. If a bitch should squash a puppy between her back and the sides of the box it is likely to scream loudly enough to bring human help or to make the bitch move.

The modern surface on which the bitch whelps is a 100 per cent polyester fur blanket. Breeders have long been seeking an alternative to the slippery secondhand newspaper, which was all that was available for many years. People have tried sacking, corrugated cardboard, old towels and blankets, but each had disadvantages. The problem is to give the bitch the degree of sleeping comfort she is used to while affording the puppies some grip for their uncertain limbs, and also to provide fabric that can be easily washed and will act as a one-way nappy for the quite copious puppy urine and also the bitch's secretions. Now we have fur beds, a development of a fabric used in human hospitals for the very ill and incontinent patient. They are strengthened for animal use and have a fairly stiff canvas-like backing so that they lie in place. All fluids drain through it onto a pad of newspaper so that the fur never becomes wet. The fur pile is one inch high so that the puppies can grip when crawling towards their dam to feed, and the surface is so warm and comfortable that it relaxes the bitch and makes her content to stay with the pups. Before this, it was sometimes difficult to convey to the pet bitch that she must leave the comfort of the settee and lie on a bed of newspaper to whelp and to tend her pups. Although the fur is snow-white, in order to avoid any toxic dye, it is resistant to all stains, and washes and dries very quickly. Most breeders find that they can manage with two pieces to fit their box, and many are now saying that fur beds has entirely altered the pattern of whelping.

The chief worry about whelping on newspaper is that as each puppy is born it brings with it a considerable quantity of fluid which drenches earlier arrivals that are already dry, so causing fluctuations of temperature which are very dangerous for a puppy trying to adjust to conditions outside the womb. One remedy is to remove the earlier puppies to a separate box, but this is not a wise thing to do as it distresses the bitch and hinders the whelping, for the bitch's uterine contractions are increased and the birth of the rest of the litter speeded up from the bitch's tending and feeding puppies already born. Fur beds make it possible for all the litter to be warm and dry around the bitch. If polyester is washed carefully, by machine or hand, it can afterwards be used as normal bedding or kept in reserve for use as a special comfort in illness.

Your next requirement is some pieces of old, discardable, towelling on which to dry the puppies; blunt ended scissors; small pieces of gauze; a thermometer; and lots and lots of newspaper to put under the fur bed and to cover the run when the puppies are older.

There is always a slight risk that your bitch may not come into milk at once or may not produce enough to feed a big litter, or that her teats may be too large to be operative for newborn puppies. You will need to be prepared with a premature baby bottle, bottle brush, sterilizing jug, and a small quantity of bitch replacement milk. It is a good idea to have this feeding kit in hand and not use it, than be in a panic to obtain it, as its constituent items are not in regular demand and so may not be stocked by your neighbourhood shops.

Looking ahead to the happy time when your puppies are running about, you will need some barricades to form a run for them as they will do an awful lot of damage to the home if they are allowed to run free. If you plan to use old doors, be sure that they are not covered in paint containing lead, which can be fatally toxic if the wood is chewed, as it is likely to be. Panels of weldmesh edged with cheap wood, which can be hooked together, have served us well; thinner wire has been gnawed into holes but would serve for the smaller breeds. However, weldmesh is very difficult to clean when little puppy paws smother it with faeces, so rigid plastic sheeting might be better. Plan to have a fairly big run as puppies coming up to selling time need to be able to play and be active.

It is also a good idea to stock up on Kennel Club forms (for registering your puppies) and pedigree forms, the latter being available at big dog-shows or by post from the offices of the weekly dog papers. You should also be planning to have a diet-sheet typed and duplicated and as much information as you can gather on your breed and the way to care for it and bring it up, so that you can give all this knowledge to those who buy your puppies.

You will find that bitch and puppies take a fair share of your life. You will want to be with the bitch in the days preceding and after the birth and, once the puppies start to be weaned, you will want to be in almost constant attention. At selling time you must be available to interview customers, who must be allowed to spend several hours with bitch and puppies while you assess them for suitability as new owners. You will find the litter very demanding, very hard manual work, but a most rewarding experience.

Looking forward to Whelping

The last few days before whelping will find your bitch very fidgety and uncomfortable if she is carrying a big litter. The teats will have enlarged and become distinctly separated, and she may require tempting to eat as appetite is reduced owing to her bulk.

It is a sensible plan to take her to visit the veterinary surgeon so that he can check that all is well and probably predict the nearness of the whelping day. This is the time to find out what his arrangements are for emergency calls, how to reach him at night and at weekends, and who will be on duty at the time you may require help. You must also find out about dew-claw removal and tail-docking if it applies in your breed. The position is that hardly anyone is able to justify the mutilation of tiny puppies by the removal of part or all of their tails on what is only the whim of fashion. While a full tail may impede a working dog, the vast majority of pedigree animals are never required to work and may just as well bear a full tail. One can see no reason at all for docking the tail in my own breed, the Boxer, and yet we do it, for not to conform to the Kennel Club standard might prejudice the puppies against getting the right sort of home, for people like a dog that conforms with those they have seen in pictures. Veterinary surgeons have been told by their ruling body that tail-docking is to be deplored, but have not been forbidden to perform the operation, so the usual ploy is to try to persuade the owners to leave tails on, certainly in companion stock of Yorkies, Cockers and Poodles where the outline is hardly affected. Very few vets will dock cross-breeds in order to make them look like one breed or another; doing that does seem a needless cruelty when the dog cannot ever hope to fulfil show criteria. If you insist that your puppies must be docked and dew-clawed, most veterinary surgeons will perform the operation when the puppies are a few days old, certainly before a week has passed. Failing this, you can arrange for an experienced breeder to do the tails and claws; this is quite legal before the puppies' eyes are opened.

This seems the appropriate time to discuss caesarean section, the surgical means by which your puppies may have to be born if the bitch is unable to produce them normally. The reasons for caesarean removal of puppies are usually:

One or more of the pups is grossly over-size and cannot get through the cervix to be born.

A puppy has moved into such a position that it is completely blocking the progress of the others.

The bitch has inertia, i.e. she has stopped having expelling uterine contractions, either because she is tired or because of a hereditary tendency to be unwilling to expel pups, as occurs in some breeds.

There is some gross infection of the uterus, possibly caused by a dead puppy, which makes it imperative to salvage the others.

A road traffic accident has injured the heavily pregnant bitch.

A large-headed breed where caesareans are almost customary, e.g. the Boston Terrier or the French Bulldog.

Caesarean section is rarely required in the cross-bred bitch. A caesarean operation consists of surgically opening the abdomen, taking out the full uterine horns, and removing the puppies and probably placentae too. The puppies are cleaned and dried by an assistant and the bitch is sutured by the veterinary surgeon. If this one episode of breeding is enough for you, it might seem logical to spay the bitch at the same time, but this is not done if it can possibly be avoided as all the parts are very much enlarged and the degree of shock is much greater than if it is done when the bitch is not pregnant.

A caesarean is now a relatively safe operation, but it is an expensive way of delivering puppies. The worst thing to do is to fear a caesarean so much that you let your bitch go on struggling to produce by the normal route, so that she comes to caesarean totally exhausted and having put the puppies at risk for too long; for they will die if they are not born soon after they separate from the uterus. You run the risk of losing the bitch and she will almost certainly not produce live puppies if labour has gone on for more than eight hours without producing a puppy. It is better to disregard expense, to get help, and elect for caesarean soon after an obstruction becomes apparent, rather than wait and lose puppies that had every chance of being strong. It follows that you may need your vet to perform a caesarean in late evening or during the night, so you must know how to get in touch with him at all times. Veterinary surgeons in Britain are obliged by their governing body to give a 24-hour service, and while this is not possible for one man, you will find that they all have a covering service with other veterinary surgeons nearby.

Any anaesthetic given to the bitch for surgery will pass to the puppies, so they will be less active than normal for 24—36 hours after they are born. Pups should be put on to the bitch while she is still semi-conscious, otherwise she may reject them as she will not have the normal reactions if they have not been born by the normal route.

Most caesarean incisions are made in the midline of the body, and this does not seem to cause wound breakdown even when the pups are pulling on the teats. The alternative is a flank incision. It is best not to quarrel with the vet's choice as he operates best by a familiar route. The charge for caesarean is often equated to the selling price of one puppy.

A dead puppy which is blocking the route of others can sometimes be removed by forceps, but an eminent veterinary surgeon has said that he has never got one out alive by this method. Forceps and other instruments should never be used by lay personnel, it is all too easy to injure the vagina of the bitch.

Your last task in the run-up to whelping week is to resist issuing invitations to view! Many people are curious and fascinated to see a birth, from those who feel it would be instructive for children, to those young mums who missed the best part of their own production number. You are well advised to refuse to have any company except for one experienced breeder friend if you are not confident of your own ability. As has been emphasized earlier, it is a very private and primitive time for the bitch, when she would by choice take herself off to be quite alone. Bitches are quite capable of holding up their whelping if there are too many people around and it would be a pity to run into the drama of a caesarean just through giving friends an educational treat. Even people the bitch knows and likes should be excluded, and the attendants restricted to at the most two people and the vet if needed. The same team should be the only ones to have access to bitch and puppies for at least two weeks after the birth. If you badly want the children of the household to see a puppy born, wait until nearing the end of the whelping before calling them in as the bitch may feel somewhat easier when she has produced some puppies.

It is true that some bitches do surprise their owners and are found in the morning with litter complete, warm, and dry, without any help at all, but with the pedigree bitch this situation is rare.

The Whelping

As whelping time draws near you will see that the bitch's vulva is enlarging and softening and that the white discharge is becoming more profuse. Inside the uterus the puppies will be revolving from the position they have grown in, on their backs, to a head- or tail-down position for their journey into the world.

The bitch may refuse food or vomit what she has eaten and if you have kept a twice daily temperature chart for the previous week you will find the temperature down by about two degrees as whelping draws near. The bitch may begin to shiver and to make an incessant panting which can go on for over eight hours in some breeds. It is very exhausting both for owner and bitch but seems to be necessary and cannot be stopped; it is an absolutely normal happening. During this stage the cervix, which has been tightly sealed with a mucous plug during pregnancy, will dilate and start to open to allow the passage of puppies; the mucous will gradually emerge from the vulva. During this phase most bitches have the urge to tear with mouth and paws. We used to call it bed-making but now informed opinion indicates that it is a reaction to pain that makes the bitch do this and not an urge to make a bed. If possible allow the bitch to tear up newspaper or some waste material as it is a pity to frustrate her, but do not risk her with upholstered furniture or her fur bed. The uterine contractions are at first involuntary and seem to cause the bitch some pain or at least distress. The main thing to look out for at this stage is a green-stained discharge at the vulva. If you get this, before any puppy has been born, there is reason to worry and to call help. Green discharge *after* one or more puppies are born is normal. The green stain comes from the separating edge of the placenta.

There is need for the puppies to be born quite quickly after the placenta has detached from the wall of the uterus, because at this stage they are in a sort of no-man's-land. Having given up dependency on the dam, the sooner they get out of their protective bags and start to breathe into their own lungs the better; inhaling mucous inside the bag is dangerous. Each puppy is attached by its own placenta, the liver-like blood-filled piece of tissue that will come out with the puppy or just after it. Each puppy is enclosed in two layers of fine skin bag, the outer one, the Chorio Allontoic Membrane, being filled with liquid, mostly puppy urine, which acts as a cushion and propellant of the puppy as the uterus contracts and squeezes the puppy on its way up over the pelvis, through the cervix, and down the straight of the vagina plop out onto the floor of the whelping box. We call this bag of fluid the 'water bag'; it is blackish in colour and will be the first thing you see emerging from the greatly enlarged vagina. Many bitches stand to deliver and their puppies will literally fall out.

The water bag may appear at the vulva and come and go for a while, then it will break, or the bitch will break it by licking, and there will be a gush of fluid into the box. It may be another two hours before the first puppy is born; some 40 per cent of pups are born feet first, so common as to be almost normal, but head first is easier, particularly with the first puppy which has to blaze the trail. The head on a puppy is conveniently wedge-shaped and its fur helps to sleek it along; the shoulders are the widest part and once they are through the cervix, descent into the world should be easy. A puppy coming feet first puts up a certain amount of resistance and its head is in its bag longer, so it must be opened and revived particularly quickly.

After many hours of deep, worrying panting, the bitch will become more quiet; she may still shiver with emotion. At this time you should be watching closely for the first deep expulsive contraction.

Veterinary surgeons like to know when a whelping is imminent so that they may arrange for someone to be available should help be needed. If your bitch starts the pre-whelping panting behaviour during the day or evening up to 10 p.m., it is as well to advise the vet, but if she begins whelping behaviour during the night there is no need to alert the vet, unless she has progressed into strong contractions but has not been able to expel a puppy. Another occasion for seeking advice might be when the bitch has been experiencing unproductive contractions for some hours and then ceased to make any effort.

In America large veterinary hospitals usually have some personnel actively on duty all night. In Britain, the Royal College of Veterinary Surgeons requires its members to be on call for 24 hours a day, but it is not customary for the vet to sit up waiting for emergencies. Provision is always made for telephone contact, and for cover by other practices if one vet is ill or away. Reluctant as you may be to wake a tired vet, if you are a novice at whelping I think you should give the welfare of your bitch priority and get help if you feel it is needed.

At the first pain the novice bitch may give a little cry, and look round at her flanks to see what is hurting. Your rôle is to stroke her and tell her she is a good, clever girl. Note the time of her pain because this is important to the vet if he has to take any action. The big pain will be followed by a few further spasms. Now either the water bag and the puppy move down or there is a hold up and the bitch stops straining. We hope that you will see the water bag, and that it is followed by the puppy, within say 45 minutes.

It is likely that a grossly enlarged bitch will not be able to reach round to her hindquarters, or she may not realize what she has to do, so you must be ready to help. Break the bag enclosing the puppy with blunt scissors, or your finger-nails. Never mind if the placenta is still attached; that can wait until you have the puppy breathing. With the gauze swabs, wipe round the nostrils and inside the mouth, and hold the puppy's head down so that any mucous can drain out. Do all this beside the bitch so that she can lick and help, and not fear that you are taking away this object that has already caused her a lot of trouble.

The pup should give a cry at this stage and you may now turn to separating it from the placenta, if the bitch has not done so. With your fingers, smooth up the tube towards the puppy so that it gets any blood remaining in the umbilical cord, then with the scissors, or again with sharp nails, break the cord as near the placenta as possible, leaving a long end attached to the puppy. You have no need to suture, or tie, and in any case such action is said to induce

Corner of garage partitioned and made draught free, so that temperature of whelping area can be raised without undue expense

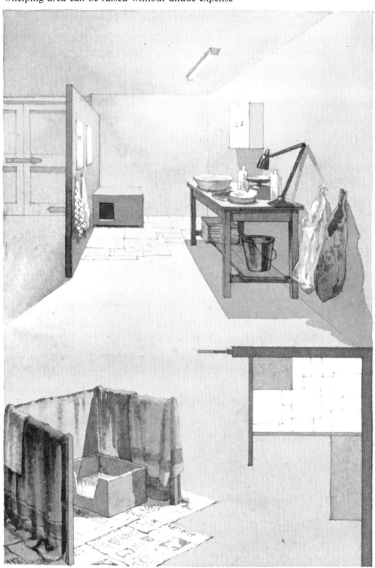

Plan of garage corner with barrier to prevent puppies escaping at 4-8 week stage

Puppy in its double lined sac appearing at the vulva

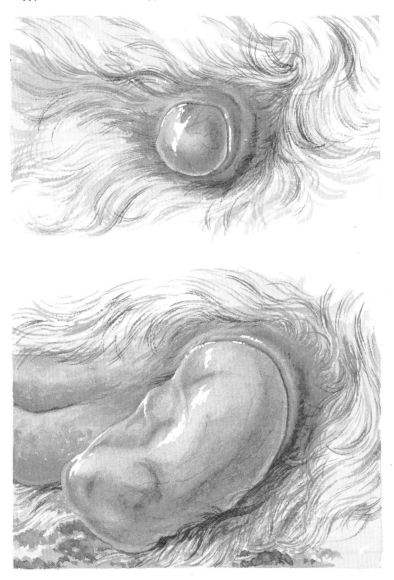

umbilical hernia. The long cord will wither and drop off within a few days.

The puppy will be wet and it will be your joint objective, you and your bitch, to get it dry as quickly as possible. The bitch will be anxious to lick the anus so that the pup passes its first faeces. Then the puppy may be put on to a teat; the milk may have been present for some days, or may not have let down yet, but the sucking action of the pup will help production.

It would be nice to be able to say that this performance will be repeated in x minutes or y hours, and that any longer interval means you must telephone the vet, but unfortunately it is impossible to be so precise, as each individual whelping pattern is different, and you can only estimate progress by watching your bitch closely. Some bitches have a little sleep between puppies and a natural interval of nearly two hours, others will shell out pups at twenty-minute intervals; or the patterns may be mixed, in that you will get a long hold up and then two puppies quite quickly. We do not know if they come alternately from each horn or whether one empties first; we do know that hitting the cervix dead in the middle and a nice vigorous contraction right after is the smartest way to get born.

The bitch usually wants to comply with the intentions of nature and eat the placentae; but being blood-filled they will cause loose bowel movement at a time when it would be inconvenient for her to leave her puppies. The best solution is a compromise: take away as many placentae as you can (usually the early ones) and let the bitch eat the ones from the last arrivals. By then she will be quite mobile and will probably manage to seize them anyway. Placentae are best flushed down the lavatory.

There are two main kinds of arrest in whelping, one when the bitch is straining hard but producing nothing, symptoms of an obstruction; and the other when the bitch is just doing nothing, a sign of inertia.

Strong straining pains should not be allowed to go on over an hour; at this point you must telephone the vet and tell him what has happened so far. Complete inactivity is a worrying phenomenon at two hours unless the bitch is resting very quietly; sitting up, fussing, but not straining, says 'Inertia' to me. Your veterinary surgeon can help by giving the bitch an injection of an ecbolic which will set up contractions in the uterus within twenty minutes or so. This drug should only be given by a veterinary surgeon as the action could be disastrous if there is an obstruction. Ecbolics are short acting and usually have effect only on one puppy. Having produced one by this means the bitch may go on by herself. It may be that the puppy she has produced is dead, but its removal will give later ones the chance of getting out alive.

It is a very sound practice to keep a detailed log of the timings of your bitch's whelping as this could be extremely useful for comparison at another time.

Breeds vary a good deal in the times they take to whelp and it would seem that the plain-shaped dogs, the labradors and beagles, give birth easily, while boxers and bulldogs are among the slowest. This may be because of the heavy-fronted, slim-waisted construction of these breeds. It is said that passing a towel under the waist, and pulling up on the ends can just help to push a puppy up and over the pelvis in these breeds.

Do not be too disturbed if your veterinary surgeon suggests that you drive the bitch into the surgery for examination and treatment. If surgery is to take place it will be necessary, and it often happens that if there is inertia, the drive will trigger the bitch off to start pushing again. Keep her warm on the journey, preferably with someone in the back to observe and hold her steady. It might be that your next puppy is born at the traffic lights! Sometimes a little walk round the garden may get a lazy bitch working again, but if you try this at night, take a torch because you may find that when she squats to urinate a puppy pops out and it would be awful to leave it behind.

We hope that at your first whelping there are no traumas and that a moderate number of puppies are born at discreet intervals. So how do you know when the bitch has finished? Again, no patent way to tell. There is a certain peace and contentment that comes over bitch and litter, when the bitch will lie on her side, the puppies all dry and feeding, and you cannot but conclude that the births are all over. It may be this way, but some nervous bitches will continue to fuss even when all the action is past.

I consider it essential to have a bitch examined by a veterinary surgeon within 24 hours of conclusion of whelping, if she looks calm and content; and much sooner if I have any doubt about her condition.

Those researching the problems of the brood bitch tell us that it is unrealistic to expect a whole litter to be born alive when bitches have so many puppies. There are many reasons why puppies are born dead, including some infection of the bitch during pregnancy; a slight bruising; or malformation of the foetus in some way; often one that is not visible to the eye such as a heart defect. Do not grieve for dead puppies or for those that have to be put down because of an obvious defect.

It is also best not to keep any puppies that are not of standard colour or markings for your breed. It does seem cruel to 'waste' these pups at the time, but experienced breeders have found that it is very often the non-standard pup that comes into rescue services. The reason is not absolutely clear cut, but probably a combination of mis-marked puppies being sold more cheaply, and lack of pride in having the 'right type'. I have kept puppies with very obvious faults in the past, including one born with only one eye, and have had the greatest difficulty in getting homes for them. People buying pedigree dogs are buying beauty and perfection and I would rather destroy a malformed puppy at birth than risk it being unwanted later.

If you should have the terrible misfortune to lose your bitch at whelping you will want to have a try at handrearing the puppies, though it is the most exhausting job known to the dog-breeder, involving two-hourly bottle-feeding day and night for the first fortnight, as well as all the toileting the bitch would normally do. Even the best bottle régime will give digestive problems. If the bitch has little or no milk, you can nevertheless make your task easier if she is available and willing to clean up the puppies and help exercise them. Bottle-fed puppies are weaned sooner than others and can be very people-orientated and affectionate.

One more expelling contraction by the bitch delivers the puppy still enclosed in its bags. Note the green stain made by the amniotic fluid released from births of earlier puppies

An experienced bitch will tear off the membranes surrounding the puppy. It is normal for her to eat all the debris at whelping time and also to consume puppy faeces and urine for 3-4 weeks after the birth

A newly delivered puppy gasps its first breath of the outside world. The bag in which it was born still surrounds the lower half of the body and the placenta is still attached by the umbilical cord

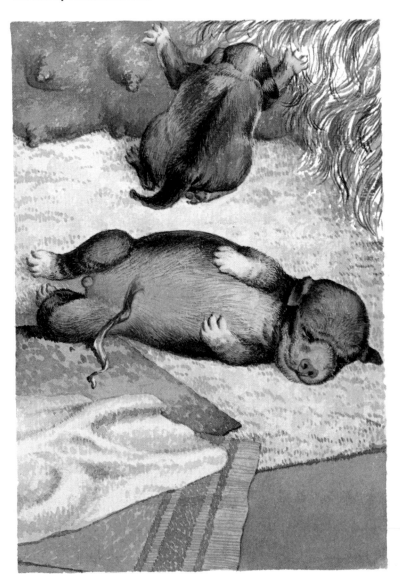

The bitch licks her new born puppy to dry it, and also to stimulate its internal organs into action

After the Whelping

When you judge the whelping to have finished, your first task will be to get the bitch outside to be clean while someone else removes the soiled fur bed and the soaked paper underneath and puts in clean layers of papers and a fresh fur bed. The soiled one van be washed by hand or machine and will be completely dry, stainless, and ready to use again in a few hours. We find that even tiny puppies protest strongly by whining and crying if they are put on a different surface, so you need at least two pieces. You will find it quite difficult to get the bitch outside, and may even have to put a collar and lead on to drag her, but she will need to be clean, so insist she stays long enough for that duty. If you give in about being clean you will find she holds out as long as she dares and then deposits on your floor, for even house-training rules can be disregarded in her opinion, if they require her to leave her precious puppies. Scrutinize what she does in the garden; she may still drop another puppy or a placenta.

Bitches that have just whelped or are feeding puppies are best confined to their own gardens; other dogs will be attracted to their scent much as they are to a bitch in season, and there is always the chance of infection at a vulnerable time if you take her out in public.

Most bitches like drinks of water throughout the whelping, especially during the panting phase, but they seldom eat. After whelping she will be glad of a good meal and I like to make it something special. If she has eaten a quantity of afterbirths, meat will not be wanted; so then I might give madeira cake or some sweet biscuits, an egg custard, or perhaps chicken. The meal will have to be offered in the whelping box, and so will copious draughts of water, for the bitch will not get out if she can help it in these early days. While she is eating you may take the opportunity to wash the fur on her hindquarters and dry her again so that the coat is not stained. Water must be offered frequently in addition to any milky drinks you may care to give. The bitch should be fed little and often for the first few days after whelping, as she has yet to settle down again to a normal digestive pattern; her organs may have been considerably displaced when she was carrying the puppies. Feed according to demand, but do not stuff her, for the puppies will not yet be taking a large quantity of milk and she will be getting almost no exercise.

The bitch will have a discharge from the vulva, blackish/red for the first 36 hours, gradually paling to bright red, the discharge coming from the sites in the uterus where the placenta separated. The discharge may go on for some weeks if a big litter was born; this is normal, provided the discharge is clean and does not smell. Any continuance or return to a black, tarry, offensive discharge needs quick veterinary attention, certainly within an hour or two because something is going wrong indeed; there may be something decaying within the uterus.

Handle your puppies gently, looking for any malformations; it may be some days before deformities become apparent. Check each day to see that navels are dry and healthy, and also dew-claws and tails after docking. A word about the docking operation: If your vet comes to the house to do them, we find it best to remove one or two puppies at a time to be docked in another room as far from the bitch as possible, because they scream when cut. We let these pups recover in a box on a hot water bottle until all sign of bleeding has stopped and then return them to the mother, and then take another pair. It is time-consuming but avoids the tremendous upset to the bitch that the removal of the whole litter brings. If a lactating bitch is stressed in any way it can take a long while to settle her again, so I try to avoid it.

Many people believe in weighing little puppies every day so that you can see that they gain; others can judge just by looking at them and by the feel. They should be full and solid, not limp and chilly to touch. Test the bitch's teats to see that all have a milk-flow; milk is increased by the sucking action of the puppies. If you feel that any of the puppies are not getting sufficient feeding, it is a good idea to make up a bottle feed and to offer it to any puppy that needs it. Those that are full will reject the idea quite forcibly. Twice a day is enough for supplementary feeding, which should only be necessary for the first few days. It is better to feed a little all round rather than remove some puppies for bottle-feeding. Complete bottle-feeding without the help of the dam means that you have to see that the pups pass urine and faeces after every meal, and these actions will probably have to be stimulated by massaging the abdomen with a hot, damp tissue. Feeding bottles must be cleaned and sterilized, just as for a human baby.

Look at the puppy claws; they can become hooked and very sharp. Trim them just slightly once or twice a week until the puppies are sold. The bitch can get badly scratched by the pounding of the puppies' paws when the claws are like little hooks and it may make her less inclined to feed the pups.

The bitch should at this stage spend most of the day either caring for her pups or sleeping with them; no formal exercise is necessary for her. She should lie stretched out on her side to allow all the pups maximum access to her teats. Sitting up, panting, or curling herself into a ball indicates that something is wrong. It may be something physical which the vet can remedy, or it may be a psychological dislike of puppies. Not all bitches are maternally minded, though most are; I have known bitches that were absolutely miserable when made to look after puppies, although they did not mind the actual whelping.

Your two big worries with the bitch at this time and until the puppies are weaned are *eclampsia* and *mastitis*. Be on the watch for both these diseases. Eclampsia or Lactation Tetany is caused by an imbalance of the calcium that is essential to life and that state can occur even if you have been feeding calcium quite faithfully. Sometimes there is more demand on the dam than she can process, or perhaps her body is not capable of assimilating enough calcium. The signs can vary; in my own dogs there has always been some mental involvement and bizarre behaviour, e.g. leaving the puppies and hiding under furniture, literally climbing the walls and biting at the plaster, screaming, seeing things that are not there, or total collapse. There is so much mental involvement that one is tempted to say that eclampsia is more likely to be generated in a bitch that is in some way stressed. The danger of eclampsia and the need for absolutely immediate action means that the bitch should not be left long unattended when she has young puppies. You must look at her every hour or so to see all is well. If you suspect eclampsia, get the vet at *whatever hour of the day or night* it happens, without delay. You will not be refused if you say eclampsia may be likely. An intravenous injection of calcium borogluconate will reverse the condition very quickly, but unless the bitch gets this injection she will die.

The other disaster, which is trying but less serious, is a mastitis in one of the teats. The first sign will be swelling and a hot spot, and neglect by the pups of that teat. If you notice at this stage you can help greatly by putting on hot poultices to reduce the congestion. Antibiotics may be prescribed but, remember, anything given to the bitch goes through to the puppies and may make them scour by killing off the beneficial bacteria in the intestine. If the mammary gland goes on being inflamed and becomes increasingly purple and hot, then you must get veterinary advice as you could lose all the milk and have the mammary gland split open into a

Head of puppy at 5 days old

3 week old puppy's head

Detail of newly born pup's ear

56

Feeding puppy by means of Belcroy Premature Baby feeder. Limbs should be free to allow puppy ability to make normal kneading and kicking movements

painful ulcer. Vigilance is the best policy, over both bitch and puppies, so that you notice any diseased condition at an early stage, before it becomes more serious.

The puppies' eyes should open about ten days after birth; at first they will look like little slits. The eyes should be clean, but if there is any stickiness, bathe them free, twice a day. All eyes are blue at first and change as the puppy grows. Puppies hate bright light and because of this we maintain a twilight atmosphere in their room.

From ten days after the birth onwards the bitch will be eating more; I usually feed her according to appetite, for it is almost impossible to give too much. My bitches receive the food they are normally used to, but three to four times as much, with vitamins and minerals in proportion. A lactating bitch who will not eat is a worry; she must be coaxed. If she misses only one meal she perhaps has indigestion, resulting from the sheer volume of food that she has processed whilst being unable to take any exercise. A human digestive remedy may help at this time.

Puppies are not born with hearing; you will notice that their ears are quite primitive at birth, and they develop gradually. When they are about three weeks old, and are struggling to their feet, their hearing is very sharp indeed. By now they can also bark.

An episode of Fading is much dreaded by experienced breeders, but is rarely met with in a novice's litter. This suggests that the phenomenon is caused by a disease that becomes indigenous where dogs have been kept and bred for a long time. It happens like this: puppies that appear to have been born healthy suddenly stop feeding, become chilled, and die in convulsions. Usually several puppies or even the whole litter become affected. It is seldom possible to treat such puppies, but a veterinary surgeon should be shown the bodies in case there is anything to be noticed that might help to prevent a recurrence.

Toxocara Canis

Recently much publicity has been given to the danger of humans, particularly children, becoming infected with the roundworm larvae from *toxocara canis,* a worm excreted mainly by puppies and nursing bitches. The danger has been greatly exaggerated but, as even one case is too many, we have to take the greatest care to ensure that puppies are free of worms, that all excreta are cleared up quickly, and that tiny children are not allowed to sit in with bitches and their litters, and if they have touched puppies or played in gardens where there are very young litters, that hands and faces are thoroughly washed. Nearly all puppies are infected by roundworm at or soon after birth. It is difficult to avoid, for most bitches have within their tissues roundworm larvae that are quite inactive until a certain stage of pregnancy impels the larvae to move across the placentae to the puppies where they develop in the lung tissues. During the first three weeks of life the puppy will cough up these larvae which then are taken down into the intestine where they will have developed into mature roundworms by the time the puppy is about three weeks old. They continue to develop, in both puppies and bitch, so that there is a continual supply. The bitch will clean up puppy faeces, so reinfecting herself, and the pups may pick up more from her coat and from her mammary glands. The bitch and her puppies are little round-worm factories and we have to get rid of their output as soon as possible.

If a drug was available that would clear encysted toxocara larvae from the bitch during pregnancy, we would be halfway to elimina-ting this parasite, but unfortunately there is none. However, with the aid of a grant from the British Small Animal Veterinary Association Clinical Studies Trust Fund, a veterinary surgeon in

Britain is carrying out research on the subject. At the moment, because we have this source of roundworm larvae in the bitch, it is inevitable that we shall find worms in the puppies, even if they do not show the classical signs of wasting and staring coat. The best action is to worm the puppies early and to keep on worming them, every two weeks, until they are four to five months old, when the routine can be cut down to once a month for the first year. Worming is trouble-free and painless, and dogs are no longer starved before receiving the dose. There is no need to fear worming.

Toxocara canis larvae are not infective to humans at the time they are passed in fresh faeces. They take some days or weeks to mature, depending on temperature and climatic conditions, and they may during that time be spread far and wide by the action of wind and rain. So it is not always those nearest to dogs who run the risk of being infected. The remedy is to clear up all puppy and bitch faeces and burn them or put them into the sewage system as soon as passed, and to keep all puppy equipment, the whelping box and any puppy-runs you may make, scrupulously clean. Children or adults who do swallow toxocara larvae will stand a very good chance of not being affected; even those who do have a transient infection may not notice it and it may only be proved by a blood-test which shows that the antibodies to the disease have been made at some time. It is very rare indeed that stray toxocara larvae imbeds into sensitive tissue and sets up a tumour-like structure. It is these very few cases of toxocara larvae embedded in eye tissue that make the headlines.

Puppies should be wormed for the first time at two and a half weeks. As the dose they require at this stage is very small, particularly for the toy breeds, I use a wormer made for children. This is a sweet-tasting liquid that even the smallest puppy will lick from a spoon. The dosage rate is one teaspoon to 10-lb (4.6kg) of body-weight, so a very small puppy will only get a few drops. A slight overdose is not critical as it does not cause diarrhoea. If you pick up each puppy and administer its dose starting at 8 a.m. you should see some results after the midday meal as probably you have by this time started them on a very small quantity of scraped meat. There may be adults worms in the faeces or there may be nothing to see as the larvae are invisible. In any case, wearing gloves, pick up all the excreta and burn them at once.

For the next worming, at four and a half weeks, I give pleasant-tasting tablets that the puppies will take from my hand; a great improvement on those pills that you have to force down the throat and are so easily brought back up again. The dosage rate should be as stated on the manufacturer's pack. At this stage I would also worm the bitch. Be sure to pick up anything she deposits in the garden. Repeat the wormings fortnightly and be sure to include in the feeding instructions that you give to your customers the information about worming.

If you would like certified proof that you are selling worm-free puppies you can, after three wormings, send small faeces samples to a laboratory to be analysed. Do this through the veterinary surgeon. The charge is quite small and it does show you have done your best to sell worm-free stock, a selling point where there are young children in the family of a puppy's new owners.

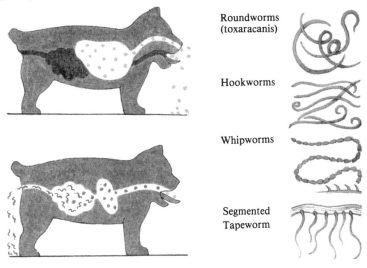

Roundworms (toxaracanis)

Hookworms

Whipworms

Segmented Tapeworm

Worms acquired via the placenta from the bitch. Larvae may be present in the puppy's lungs before birth. They are coughed up into the mouth and swallowed to enter the digestive system where they mature in the intestine and are passed out in via the faeces occasionally a heavily infested puppy may vomit an adult worm from the stomach

Puppy Environment

At about three weeks of age your puppies should be walking about, anxious to see you when you go into their room, perhaps starting to play among themselves. All eyes should be clear and open and the puppies should be able to hear. In white breeds or where there is the possibility of deafness, each puppy should be tested by dropping a metal food-tray behind it. Deaf and blind puppies often get along quite well by copying their fellows so it is important to see that each is clear of any affliction.

From 21 days onwards the puppies must socialize; to see and be handled by people, to hear household noises, the occasional crash, the radio, vacuum cleaner, and the television. My own puppy is still afraid of the foodmixer although it has been here all her life. It is a great help to the new owners of puppies if they have seen and heard all the machinery found in the modern home. The puppies can endure increasing daylight and sunshine, although you will find they huddle away from bright light and do not like the garden at this early stage. We like to move our puppies into a room that is busy, through which we pass frequently, and where they can have a run attached to their box so that their games and their messes are contained but they still have plenty of room to move about. The larger the run the cleaner your puppies will be, for you will find they move as far from their beds as possible to defaecate. Puppies kept in too cramped surroundings will never be as clean as those with reasonable freedom, but we find a run is necessary, otherwise the puppies are in danger from opening doors and their little piles and puddles are made right where you walk.

The puppies still sleep a lot and you must allow them to have all the rest they need; otherwise they will be over-stimulated and nervy. People may be encouraged to visit them, as long as they are

willing to leave the puppies alone when they collapse into a heap to sleep; puppies must not be stimulated into action like clockwork toys. The bitch should be allowed access to the puppies whenever she wishes but she must also be able to get away from them. So it is best to provide her with a bed outside their run where they cannot reach her. Once you have started to feed the puppies on meat etc., the bitch will stop clearing up their faeces. However, she will continue to feed them a little and check them over and will also start teaching them to play and to defend themselves against mock attacks.

It is most interesting to see the constructive way that a bitch will teach her puppies how to walk, how to trot and keep up with her on a circular tour of the garden, how to attack and how to get out of a nasty situation when the enemy has you in his grip. The bitch play-fights her puppies and then encourages them to attack her, sometimes letting them win the encounter and at other times scaring them so that they run away squealing but soon come back for more. This early learning must be very important to the puppy that is sold as a solitary pet, for it will probably have no further opportunity for learning in this way and its ability to defend itself in a fight may depend on what it learnt before it was eight weeks old.

The bitch's behaviour with her puppies can teach us a lot about training. If they pull her ears too hard, or if they persist in annoying her when she wants to sleep, she will snap once, decisively, and the puppies will be impressed by her anger and stop what they are doing to annoy. When the puppies approach the bitch again, she will be loving to them, she does not nag or continue to grumble. Our puppy training should be modelled on hers; a quick wallop when caught in the act and no punishment after the crime, or prolonged sulks when the puppy has forgotten what it has done.

A Dachsund bitch and her puppies

An Afghan puppy at the age at which they normally leave for new homes

Weaning the Puppies

Most people like to begin weaning by giving the puppies very small quantities of scraped beef as soon as the teeth are through, at about two and a half weeks of age. This is done even if the bitch has a good milk-flow, so that a basis for weaning has been made should the bitch have to be removed from the pups for any reason.

Scraped meat is obtained by putting a lump of meat on a board and drawing a knife down it until a pulp results. Minute balls of this meat can then be inserted in the puppies' mouths, once daily to begin with, and then twice. Minced meat is not fine enough for them at this stage, and milky meals are not acceptable while there is plenty of milk to be had from the dam. With my own dogs I do not practice early weaning as I prefer their upbringing to be as natural as possible. I would rather feed the bitch very well indeed and allow her to feed the puppies entirely until they are five weeks old, if not longer if she is able to, but always being aware that her milk may diminish, the puppies must be closely watched to see that they are satisfied. It seems to me a great pity to interfere with the mating, the whelping and the weaning anymore than is necessary for the well-being of dogs and puppies. Human food and management is not necessarily better.

As my dogs are fed on a factory formulated diet, I wean the puppies onto this kind of food, very well-soaked in warm milk, using the bitch-milk substitute for the first few weeks of weaning. This mash is put onto a flat baking tray and the puppies encouraged to dip their noses into it. I find it is no use trying to get them to feed until they can stand firmly on four legs and even then they will fall into the food, or walk through it, so the first few meals are almost entirely wasted but are nonetheless a necessary part of the learning process. If you get one puppy in the group that understands what it must do, you have achieved a lot and improvement will follow each day. I give mash once a day for two days and then twice a day, and at this stage also the puppies can be offered the palatable calcium tablets that are cheese flavoured so the puppies become attracted to them, and also multivitamin tablets. The calcium tablets may have to be broken into halves or quarters according to the size of the puppy, but they are a useful first exercise in nibbling dry substances.

When puppies are learning to feed they get quantities of sticky milk on their coats. It is useful if the bitch will still clean them but she may have given up this chore, so food should be sponged off immediately. If it dries on, not only are the puppies repulsive to look at but they may attract flies and the coat may be spoiled. When the pups are managing two milk/mash feeds daily I try giving them a third feed with meat added to the mash; fine mince with a fair amount of fat content is suitable. A range of additives can now be introduced with white fish very carefully boned, grated cheese, and carefully picked-over chicken being the favourites. From the first well-taken meal onwards I offer water several times a day. It would be nice to leave it in the puppy run but inevitably they will fall in the bowl, or turn it over, so water must be offered and then taken up. At first you will find the puppies feel they must drink it all, but gradually they learn that water is in free supply and need not be cleared up on sight.

I always feed all the puppies together from one dish as competition seems to stimulate them; it can be difficult, with a big litter, to find a dish that will accommodate all the heads at once. It is important to stand and watch the puppies feed, to observe which is hesitant or slow, and also to see if any puppy is unable to get a fair share, either from being bullied or because there is a physical complaint. You may see that one pup is coughing food up again, or that liquid comes back down its nose. Such a puppy should be marked down for very close watching for a day or so and then reported to the vet for investigation with as detailed a history of the disablement as you can provide. Disabilities do begin to show up at the time of weaning which have not been apparent before, and for your own good and peace of mind you will not want to have offered these puppies to customers and then be obliged to explain away a defect. At five weeks all puppies must be able to stand and run, to hear and see. In the short-faced breeds their breathing may still be rather noisy, but this will pass; sometimes buyers are rather worried about the puppies sounding like little engines when held close to the face, but it is quite normal.

By the time the pups are seven to eight weeks old they should be on four meals a day, every bit eaten up each time, and they should have been wormed three times.

Puppy coats change quite a lot in the first eight weeks of life. Many are born with a more fluffy coat, or a coat of different colour, than that desirable in the adult. It is useful if you can see one or two very young litters in the breed so that you know what is acceptable and normal in the new-born. People have been known to panic and threaten to discard their litters because they are not of the colour associated with the adult dog. The more knowledge you can acquire from other people's litters the better, for you will have to convince your customers that the colour or texture is developing correctly. I find that customers for Boxers seeking a strong red coat need to be shown that it is only just coming through at five weeks, for the puppies are born a rather undistinguished mouse shade.

If you intend to wean your puppies on to fresh meat and fine biscuit, you can ease the transition by thickening the puppies' milk meals with a cereal made for human babies. However, in my experience this can result (probably due to the sugar content) in too loose a bowel movement. Another method of feeding is by means of tinned meat designed to be fed with a plain biscuit meal. This is a method that appeals to the new puppy-owner, for in general tinned meats are most convenient for him to store.

A new owner will want to know feeding quantities. While puppies are in the breeder's home, feeding ad lib and communally, it is impossible to provide advance information, but in the week before a puppy is to go to a new home, I feed it separately, keeping a note of the weight of the food to give as a guide to the new owner. Separating the puppy also prepares it for dining alone in his new home, for otherwise it might suffer some loss of appetite.

You may find that when you introduce a new food puppies will show some bowel looseness, especially if it is a food with a high milk content, or with sweetening, which is also laxative. Puppies must not be allowed to endure bowel looseness because it is very weakening and dehydrating for them. So if this condition persists for more than 24 hours, get veterinary advice.

Puppies sometimes get hiccups from gulping their food. I find that gripewater is the best treatment.

Puppies will enjoy gnawing a very large marrow bone; it also helps to bring their teeth through.

Shetland Sheepdog bitch with her growing litter

Labrador Retriever bitch and her 5½ week old puppies playing in the grass

A Labrador retriever puppy at 8 weeks old

As the puppies increase their intake of food, the bitch's should be reduced; she will have been processing two, three, or even four times the normal amount of food, according to the size of litter. Her food should now be reduced and her exercise increased, and she should again be wormed. Swimming exercise is a very big help in returning the size of her teats to normal.

Many bitches shed almost all of their coats after feeding puppies. It is best to strip out what remains, and to give a bitch a good bath and trim, now that the majority of her maternal duties are over.

Selling your Puppies

You may have found, as so many of us have, that those friends who were quite sure they wanted puppies from your bitch before the mating took place no longer feel able to take them. You may not have the sexes or colours that people have set their hearts on, so it is inevitable that you will have to offer some of your puppies on the open market.

The best way to sell them in Great Britain is through the agency of Dog Breeders Associates, an organization which has been running for ten years now with the prime object of putting the public in touch with those who have puppies to sell and cutting out the puppy supermarkets where disease is apt to be rife through the indiscriminate mixing of puppies from many sources. Dog Breeders Associates (D.B.A.) charge an admission fee of £3 per annum and ask you to send £3.50 from each puppy sale you make through them. They circulate to people who enquire an up-to-date list of those who have puppies to sell; a service free to the public. Through D.B.A. you will meet people who are actively and sensibly searching for a puppy, and not the time-wasters looking for a pleasant and cheap afternoon out playing with puppies, as you may well get if you advertise locally or nationally. D.B.A. advertise widely so you may be contacted by buyers at some distance, but the expense to you is far less than it would be if you were to place your own advertisements. It is as well to get your puppies on a D.B.A. list when they are about two weeks old.

Although it takes a great deal of your time I feel it is essential and important in the long run to allow your customers to make several visits to bitch and puppies from the time they are three weeks old. Your aim is to make the ownership of their puppy a commitment for life, not an impulse buy of which they will soon tire. You have the opportunity to talk to the new owners and see what their lifestyle with the puppy will be, and whether every member of the household is wholehearted in the desire for a puppy. It can often be that a small child or an elderly relative could turn out to be the factor that makes the family unable to keep the puppy when it grows into a dog. I like to see all the members of the household if possible, but certainly husband and wife, and I never, never sell a puppy to be a surprise or present without the recipient being aware of what is coming. Surprises sometimes go terribly wrong and with a living creature one just cannot afford that.

Clients sometimes want to have a new purchase checked by a veterinary surgeon and this I am happy to allow, provided they either send their vet to my house to see the puppy, which will cost them a lot of money if they live at any distance, or take the puppy straight from my home to a vet, and bring it straight back, with a certificate signed by the vet, if there is any fault. I am not happy to have a young puppy remain in someone's house all night, possibly miserable and crying, and then be brought back, on a flimsy excuse that it did not fit in, or it puddled on the floor. It may be difficult to believe that these excuses can be offered, but there are still people who can hardly distinguish between puppies and stuffed toys.

As a dog-breeder, you really have a lifetime's responsibility for the animals you have bred. It may seem hard, when perhaps you have not seen your ex-puppy for years, that you are called upon to help people out when they have suddenly decided that they must move to a flat, or go abroad, or have another baby, and the dog must go. If a puppy of your breeding gets into a rescue scheme (and there are many run by breed societies), you will probably be telephoned the news and asked to contribute to the dog's upkeep until it is found a new home. We sometimes feel that the existence of rescue schemes makes it easy for the public to delude themselves to think that there are 'good homes waiting' for the dogs that they want to be rid of and it is all made too easy for them. Again, some people running these rescue schemes may feel that some breeders are contributing far too many dogs to the pool and are over-breeding and selling carelessly.

It is usual and sensible to take a large deposit when a puppy is definitely booked, say at the second visit of the customers when the pup is 5½−6 weeks old, the balance of the cost being payable when the puppy is collected, at 8−9 weeks. Should the deposit have been paid but the sale not concluded the deposit is returnable if you have time to sell the puppy again. If a deposit is paid but you hear no more from the customers and they do not arrive to collect the puppy and you cannot get in touch with them, then you need only keep the puppy in their names for as little as two weeks before re-selling it, but you must retain the deposit so that you can return it if the original customers turn up again. They may, when they do get in touch, say that they were counting on having the puppy and be irate that you have sold it, but the law realizes that the selling time for young livestock is very short and you are not obliged to keep a puppy 'on your shelves' in the hope of people claiming it. It is wise to state on your receipt for the deposit: 'On account of the purchase price of x pounds for *wufflehound* bitch puppy to be collected on …. January'.

If the puppy is returned to you after several weeks with a veterinary certificate for an unfitness which it is considered you should have known about, you are obliged to return the purchase price; offering another puppy is not good enough. You can be sure a veterinary certificate of this kind would not be given lightly. If the puppy is returned for any reason that is not your fault, such as another dog will not tolerate the puppy, then your best plan is to try to re-sell the puppy, deduct the new expenses you incur and a certain amount for its keep in the meantime, and return as much as you are able of the purchase price after the completion of a new sale. Older dogs which may be returned to you at around a year old when they are getting to be a nuisance because they have not been trained have absolutely no retail value at all and in fact may take you some time to rehabilitate and train, so really the owners should pay you board for the time the dog is with you.

When selling the new puppy, and we hope that all yours, in the first litter anyway, find good and permanent homes, you should provide a full diet sheet, together with information on how to feed by alternative methods in case the owners need to change later. It is kind to provide two packed meals for the puppy to take with him so that the new owners can see the amount and the texture of the food. They should be requested to keep the puppy on the same menu you have been using for the first two weeks so that he has not too much strangeness to endure. You can also recommend some books that have been useful to you, and give some hints on training, grooming and puppy development to help them. Give a certificate of worming and advise the new owners how to proceed in the future.

All puppies must be vaccinated against the four main viral diseases, but if maternal antibody has been at a good level the puppies should already be protected for up to eight weeks. It is not a good idea to have puppies innoculated before they leave you, as the primary vaccination provides a good opportunity for the new owner to make contact with a veterinary surgeon who may then be the one to look after the puppy for life. When a customer is making one of the early visits I find it is a good idea to ask him or her to contact a veterinary surgeon then and say they are thinking of getting a puppy. The vet can then advise them of the vaccination programme that he thinks will be most appropriate and tell them the cost. This seems much more satisfactory than the breeder having the vaccination done and charging extra for it on top of the cost of the puppy.

Puppy prices can be obtained by asking the stud-dog's owner, or by ringing round to check on other litters; but remember if you are going to ask a price comparable with the top kennels then you must be prepared to give the full after-care service that they do and be available for advice and help throughout the dog's life. Giving really good service will mean buying books and weekly papers, doing your reading and going to shows so that you keep up to date with knowledge; this is being a dog-breeder as opposed to just producing a litter of puppies.

I hope that the first experience may make you eager for more and that you will become one of the people who breed fine dogs to become top winners at beauty shows, to excel in the obedience world, or to fulfil their prime purpose — to be splendid companions to families and lonely people for as long as their lives shall last.

The weekly dog newspapers should be consulted for the suppliers of all equipment and products mentioned in the text.

A contented bitch and her newly whelped puppies

Puppy playpen which dismantles conviently for storage

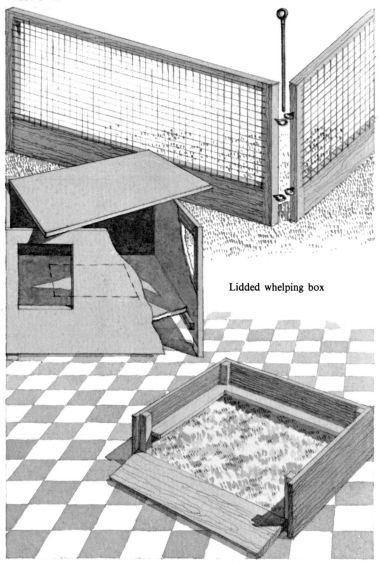

Lidded whelping box

Open whelping box for a heavily coated breed. Guard rail is shown, and front let down to form a ramp for puppies to use when they begin to walk

A fine litter of Cavalier King Charles Spaniels

Puppies are destructive at play!

Vigorous yellow Labrador puppies

Appendix

(Reproduced by the kind permission of Joint British Veterinary Association/Kennel Club)

Dogs of all breeds can be examined under this Scheme, and for each breed there is a minimum age at which a permanent Certificate can be issued. These ages vary, because P.R.A. varies in its age incidence amongst the different breeds. In the breeds in which P.R.A. is known to be a problem (see later), the age limit was decided after discussions involving the examination of case histories of very many dogs with P.R.A. In all other breeds, an arbitrary age of five years is agreed upon as the age at which a permanent Certificate can safely be issued.

Many cases of P.R.A. are apparent on ophthalmoscopic examination well before the age limits and owners are therefore encouraged to bring their dogs, in particular breeding stock, prior to the age at which a permanent Certificate can be issued, and if the dog shows no evidence of P.R.A. at that examination, a Temporary Certificate (valid for 12 months only) will be issued. In this way dogs can be used for breeding, before obtaining a permanent Certificate, with the knowledge that they have been examined and at that time showed no evidence of any hereditary eye abnormality.

The B.V.A. and the Kennel Club are very keen to eradicate P.R.A. from Britain's pedigree dogs and would like to emphasise that early examination with Temporary Certificate will go a long way towards eliminating this disease from our breeding stock as early as possible. Early examination will also reassure breeders who wish to breed from their animals long before the prescribed age at which permanent Certificate can be issued.

The issue of certificates for this Scheme is the responsibility of the British Veterinary Association and not the Kennel Club. This is done to simplify the running of the Scheme and the procedure for examination is as follows:

1.   The owner takes the dog to his own veterinary surgeon and requests that the animal be examined with a view to the issue of a certificate under the Scheme.
2.   The veterinary surgeon examines the dog and if, in his opinion, it would be worthwhile having the dog examined under the Scheme, suggests a referee from the B.V.A. Panel.
3.   The owner presents the dog to the referee, together with the Kennel Club Registration Certificate, or the Working Trials and Obedience Register acceptance, any related transfer certificates and any Change of Name Certificate.
5.   The referee examines the dog and signs the report. He then gives one copy to the owner, sends one copy to the B.V.A., and another copy to the owner's veterinary surgeon and keeps the fourth for his records. The owner should not send his copy of report form to either the B.V.A. or the Kennel Club as the issue of a certificate will be automatic if the report is favourable.
6.   A standard fee has been agreed for this examination and report by the referee. There is financial advantage in having several dogs examined at one session.
7.   The B.V.A. on receipt of the report form from the referee issues a certificate if the report is favourable.
8.   The Secretary of the B.V.A. informs the Kennel Club of those dogs for which certificates have been issued, including the name of the owner(s), for endorsement of records cards and publication in the Kennel Gazette.

HIP DYSPLASIA SCHEME:
Procedure for veterinary surgeons —
1.   The owner takes his dog(s) to his veterinary surgeon with the Kennel Club Registration Certificate(s) and, if appropriate, Transfer Certificates. He will be requested to complete and sign the B.V.A. declaration form(s). Supplies of the declaration forms are obtainable from B.V.A. headquarters.
2.   No dog may be submitted more than once to the Scheme.

3.   Minimum age for dogs entered in the Scheme is one year and the maximum age is six years.

4.   (a) The veterinary surgeon takes a radiograph of the dog's hip in the recommended position as follows:

The dog should be placed on his back, with the pelvis centred over the cassette. The hind-legs are pulled straight back, completely extending all the hind-limb joints. The legs should be parallel and each rotated slightly medially so that the patellae are located centrally over the mid-line of the femur. This forces the femur head into the acetabulum so that a true profile of the femoral head and neck will appear on the film. It is essential that the body of the dog does not roll to one side. This may be prevented by extending the forelegs and supporting the chest. (reference: Douglas, S.W. and Williamson, H.D. (1972). Principles of Veterinary Radiograph, Balliere Tindall, London. (page 119).

(b) The use of a general anaesthetic is strongly advised to facilitate positioning.

(c) In the case of large dogs, the use of a grid is essential in most cases.

(d) Left or right film markers must be used.

(e) The registration number of the dog taken from the Kennel Club registration certificate and the date the film was taken must be radiographed onto the X-ray film. No other form of identification is acceptable. The registration number required is the number which appears on the top right-hand corner of the Kennel Club Registration Certificate.

5.   The veterinary surgeon then dispatches the radiograph to the B.V.A. with the declaration form containing full details of the dog taken from the Kennel Club Registration Certificate, together with a cheque for the current fee. This fee, payable to the B.V.A., is quite separate from any fee charged by the veterinary surgeon for taking the X-ray film.

6.   A panel of three scrutineers will meet at regular intervals to examine the films.

7.   The radiograph and a copy of the scrutineers' report are then returned to the owner's veterinary surgeon with the following documents as appropriate:

(a) If the dog has passed, a B.V.A./K.C. Certificate in

duplicate, the top copy of which is passed to the owner.

(b) A 'failure' letter.

(c) For 'borderline' cases a 'breeders letter' for the veterinary surgeon to pass on to the owner.

8.   The B.V.A. will inform the Kennel Club of registered dogs which have been awarded certificates.

HEREDITARY CATARACT SCHEME:

All breeds are eligible for examination under the Joint B.V.A./ K.C. Hereditary Cataract Scheme and the age at which a permanent Certificate can be issued is indicated below. If a dog is examined prior to these age limits, a Temporary Certificate (valid for 12 months only) can be issued:

Afghan Hound	3 years
American Cocker Spaniel	5 years
Boston Terrier	18 months
Golden Retriever	6 years
Miniature Schnauzer	3 years
Staffordshire Bull Terrier	18 months
ALL OTHER BREEDS	5 years

The issue of certificates for this Scheme is the responsibility of the British Veterinary Association and not the Kennel Club. This is done to simplify the running of the Scheme and the procedure for examination is as follows:

1.   The owner takes the dog to his own veterinary surgeon and requests that the animal be examined with a view to the issue of a Certificate under the Scheme.

2.   The veterinary surgeon examines the dog and if, in his opinion, it would be worthwhile having the dog examined under the Scheme, suggests a referee from the B.V.A. Panel.

3.   The owner contacts the referee and makes the necessary appointment.

4.   The owner presents the dog to the referee, together with the Kennel Club Registration Certificate, any related Transfer Certificates and any Change of Name Certificate.

5. The referee examines the dog and signs the report. He gives one copy of the owner, sends one copy to the B.V.A., another copy to the owner's veterinary surgeon and keeps the fourth copy for his records. The owner should not send his copy of the report to either the B.V.A. or the Kennel Club as the issue of a Certificate will be automatic if the report is favourable.

6. A standard fee has been agreed for this examination by the referee. There is a financial advantage in having the examination for P.R.A. done at the same time and also in having several dogs examined at one session.

7. The B.V.A. on receipt of the report form from the referee issues a Certificate if the report is favourable.

8. The Secretary.of the B.V.A. informs the Kennel Club of those dogs for which certificates have been issued, including the names of the owners, for endorsement of record cards and publication in the Kennel Gazette.

PROGRESSIVE RETINAL ATROPHY SCHEME:

Dogs of all breeds can be examined under this Scheme, and for each breed there is a minimum age at which a permanent Certificate can be issued. These ages vary, because P.R.A. varies Minimum ages for permanent certification of breeds in which P.R.A. is known to be a problem:

At Three Years:
Border Collie, Cardigan Welsh Collie, Miniature Smooth Long-Haired Dachshund, Elkhound, Irish Setter, Rough Collie, Saluki, Shetland Sheepdog, Smooth Collie, Tibetan Spaniels, Tibetan Terrier.

At Five Years:
Cocker Spaniel, Smooth-Haired Dachshund, English Springer Spaniel, Miniature Poodle, Toy Poodle, Working Sheepdogs and cross-breds for the Obedience and Working Trials Register; all other breeds except:

At Six Years:
Golden Retrievers.

Index